D0116749

REVIEW COPY
COURTESY OF
CAPSTONE PRESS

Lexile:

LSU ☐yes
SJB ☐yes
BL: 3.6
Pts: 0.5

GRAPHIC LIBRARY™

INVENTIONS AND DISCOVERY

JAKE BURTON CARPENTER
AND THE
SNOWBOARD

by Michael O'Hearn
illustrated by Ron Frenz
and Charles Barnett III

Consultant:
Lee Crane
TransWorld Media
Oceanside, California

Capstone press®

Mankato, Minnesota

Graphic Library is published by Capstone Press,
151 Good Counsel Drive, P.O. Box 669, Mankato, Minnesota 56002.
www.capstonepress.com

Printed in the United States of America

1 2 3 4 5 6 11 10 09 08 07 06

Library of Congress Cataloging-in-Publication Data
O'Hearn, Michael, 1972–
Jake Burton Carpenter and the snowboard / by Michael O'Hearn; illustrated by Ron Frenz and Charles Barnett III.
p. cm.—(Graphic library. Inventions and discovery)
Includes bibliographical references and index.
ISBN-13: 978-0-7368-6481-7 (hardcover)
ISBN-10: 0-7368-6481-4 (hardcover)
ISBN-13: 978-0-7368-7516-5 (softcover pbk.)
ISBN-10: 0-7368-7516-6 (softcover pbk.)
1. Carpenter, Jake Burton—Juvenile literature. 2. Snowboarders—United States—Biography—Juvenile literature. 3. Snowboards—Design and construction—Juvenile literature. I. Frenz, Ron. II. Barnett, Charles, III. III. Title. IV. Series.
GV857.S57O44 2007
796.93'9092—dc22 2006008176

Summary: In graphic novel format, tells the story of Jake Burton Carpenter and the evolution of the snowboard and the sport of snowboarding.

Design
Jason Knudson

Colorist
Ben Hunzeker

Editor
Donald Lemke

TABLE OF CONTENTS

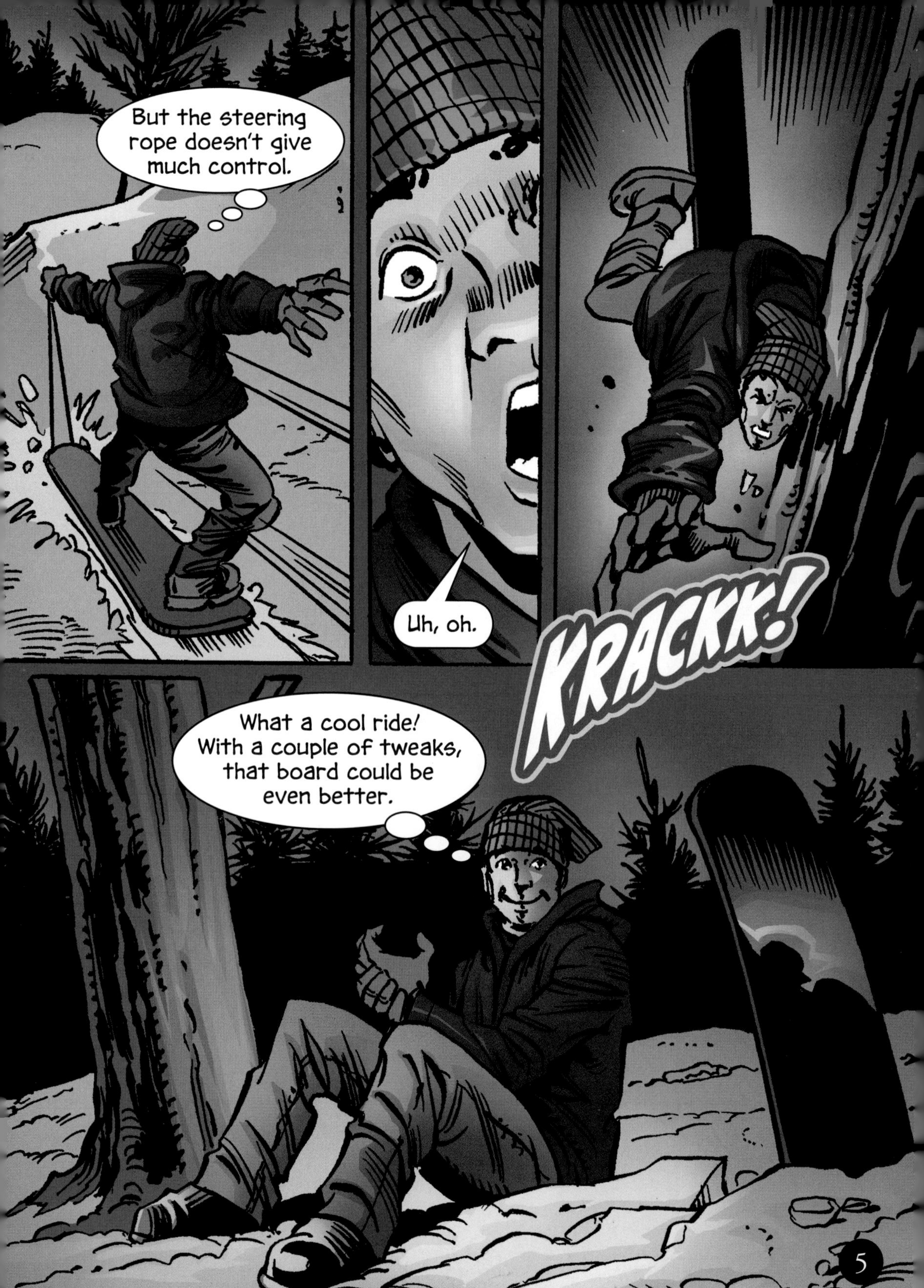

But the steering rope doesn't give much control.
Uh, oh.
KRACKK!
What a cool ride! With a couple of tweaks, that board could be even better.

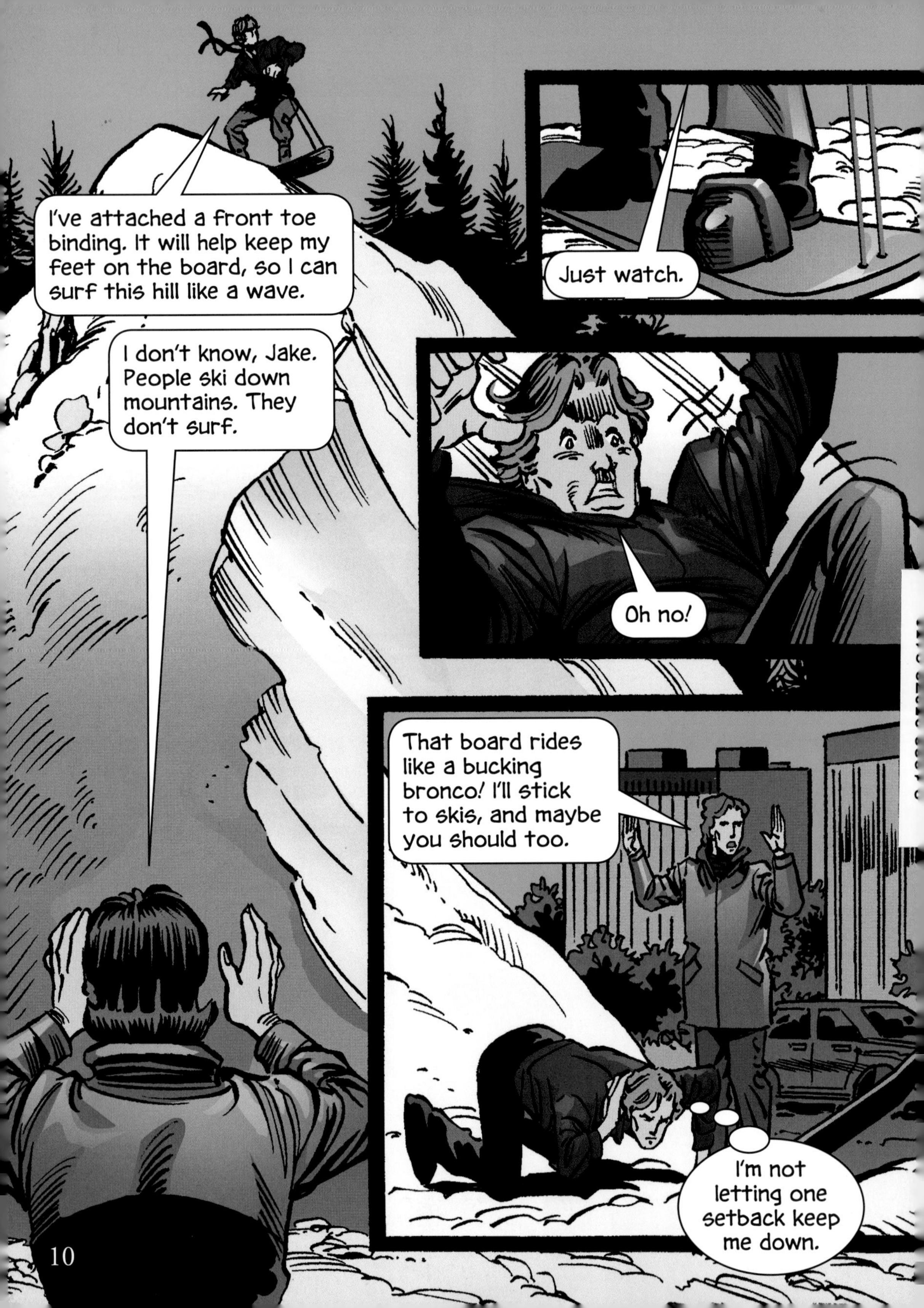
I've attached a front toe binding. It will help keep my feet on the board, so I can surf this hill like a wave.
I don't know, Jake. People ski down mountains. They don't surf.
Just watch.
Oh no!
That board rides like a bucking bronco! I'll stick to skis, and maybe you should too.
I'm not letting one setback keep me down.

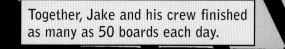

Together, Jake and his crew finished as many as 50 boards each day.

They called their creation the BBI. It became the first Burton snowboard ever sold.

Perfect. This front binding will make it more controllable than the Snurfer.

And these tail fins will really rip through the turns.

Now I just have to sell them.

13

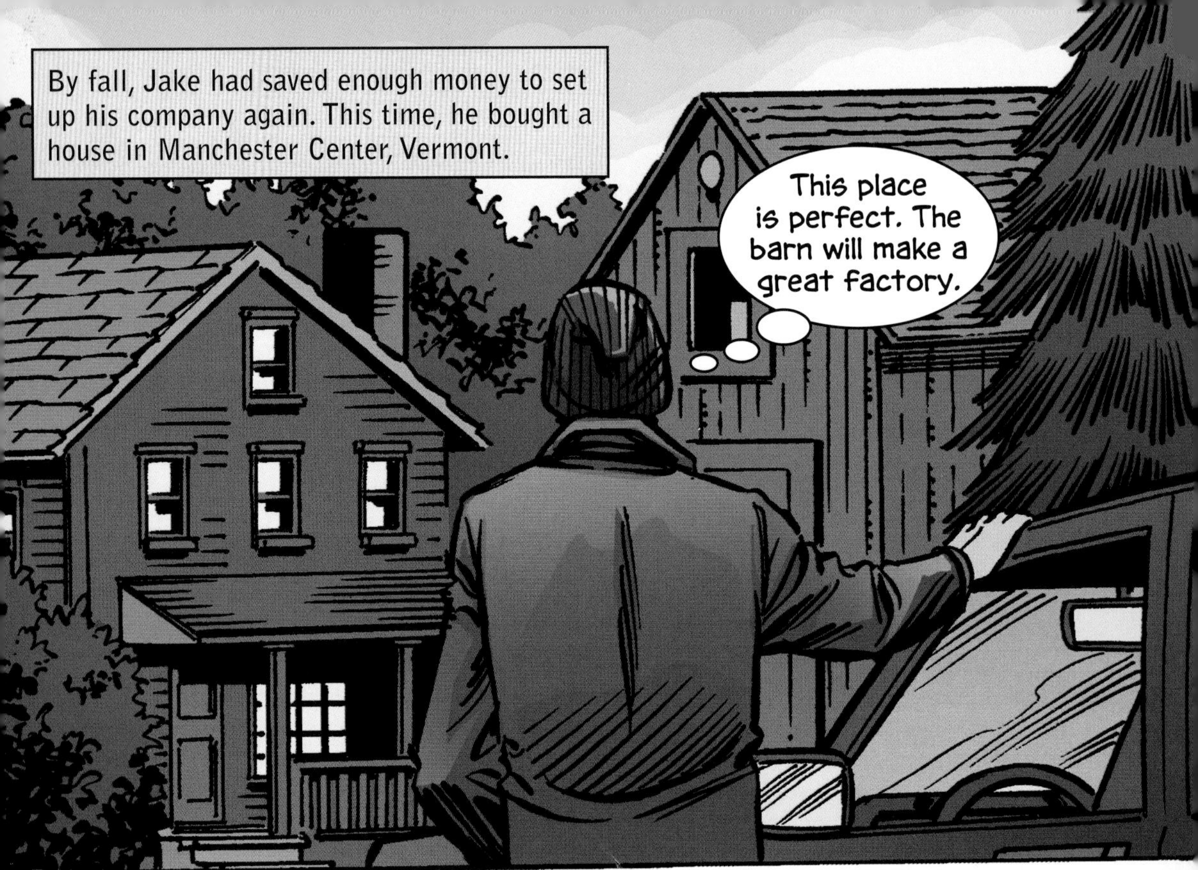
By fall, Jake had saved enough money to set up his company again. This time, he bought a house in Manchester Center, Vermont.
This place is perfect. The barn will make a great factory.

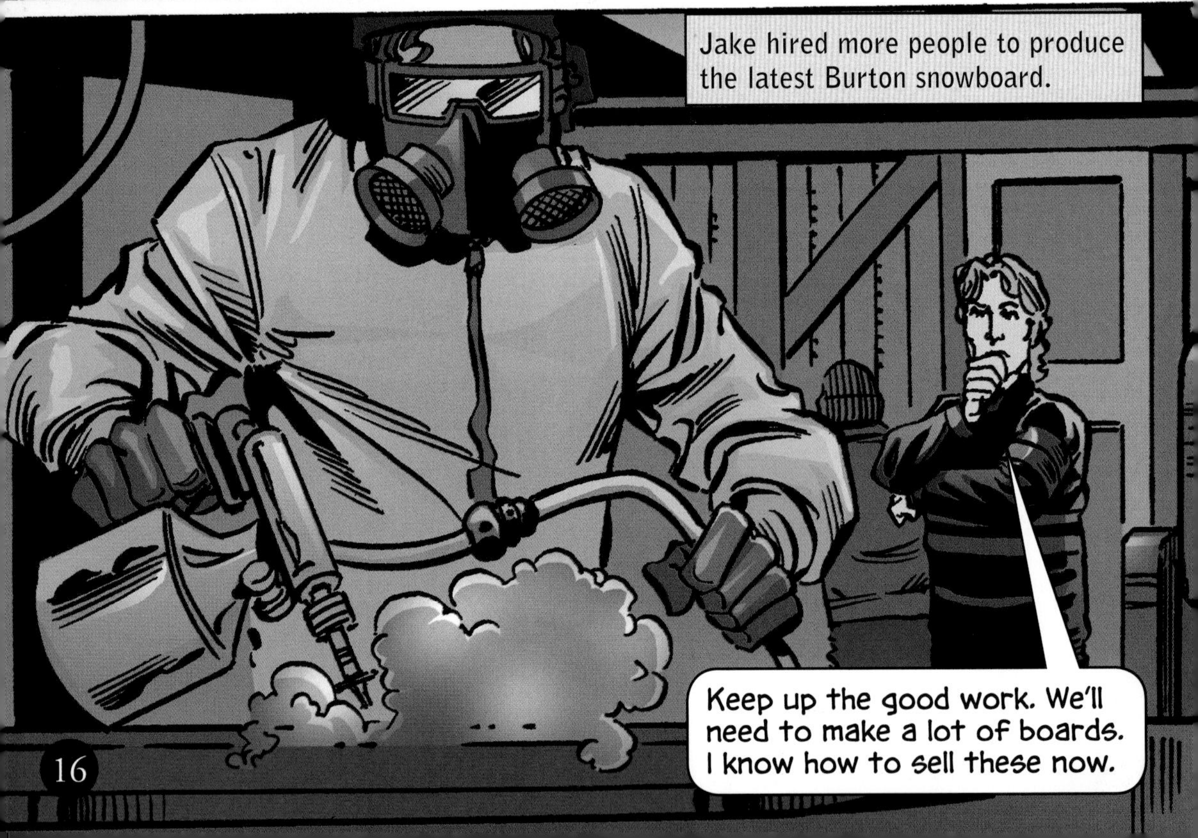
Jake hired more people to produce the latest Burton snowboard.
Keep up the good work. We'll need to make a lot of boards. I know how to sell these now.

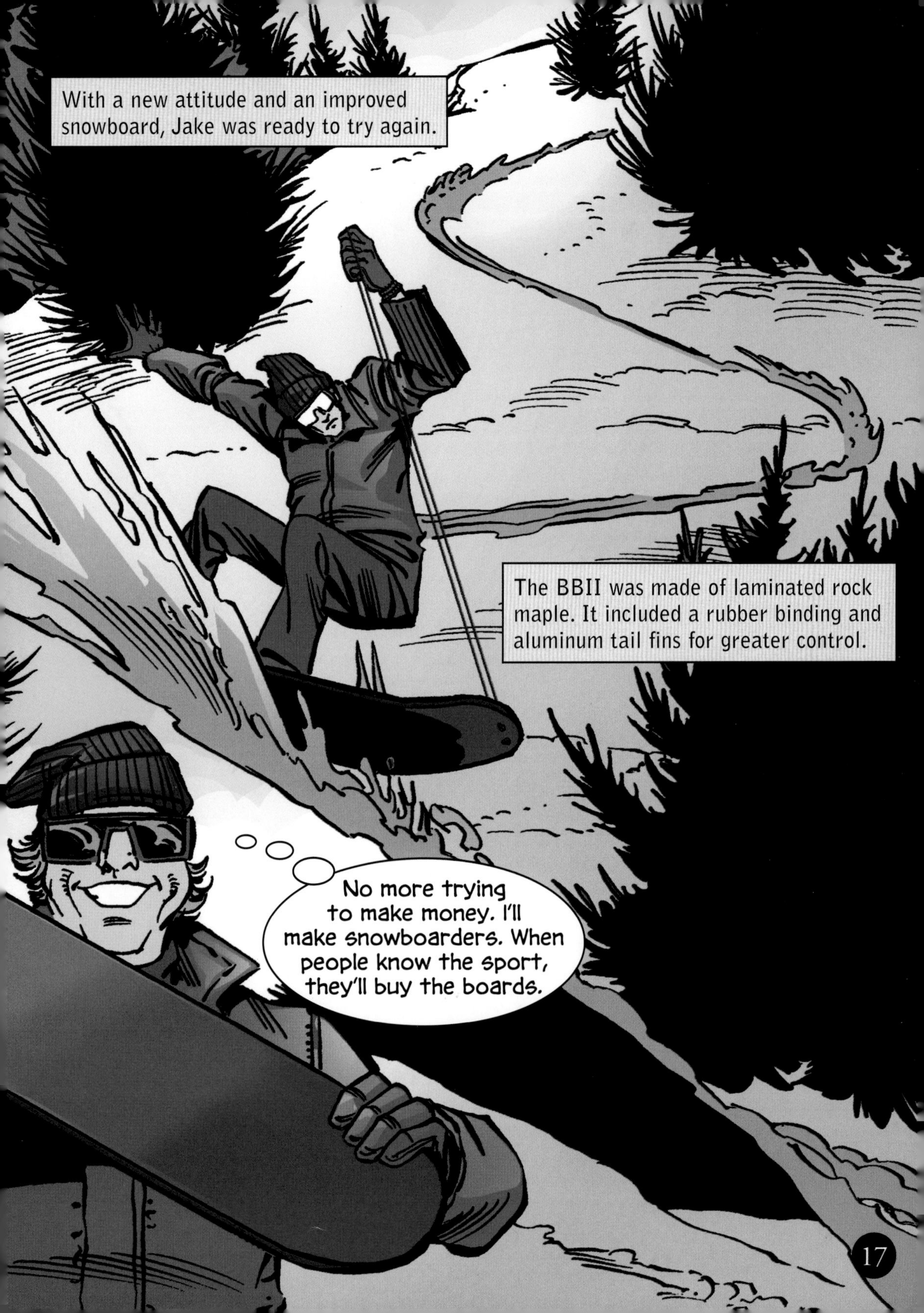
With a new attitude and an improved snowboard, Jake was ready to try again.
The BBII was made of laminated rock maple. It included a rubber binding and aluminum tail fins for greater control.
No more trying to make money. I'll make snowboarders. When people know the sport, they'll buy the boards.

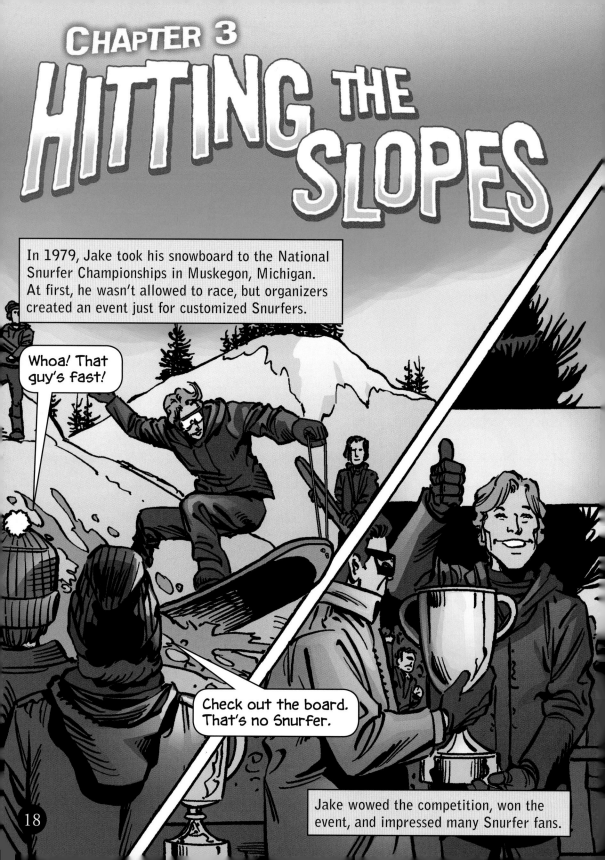

19

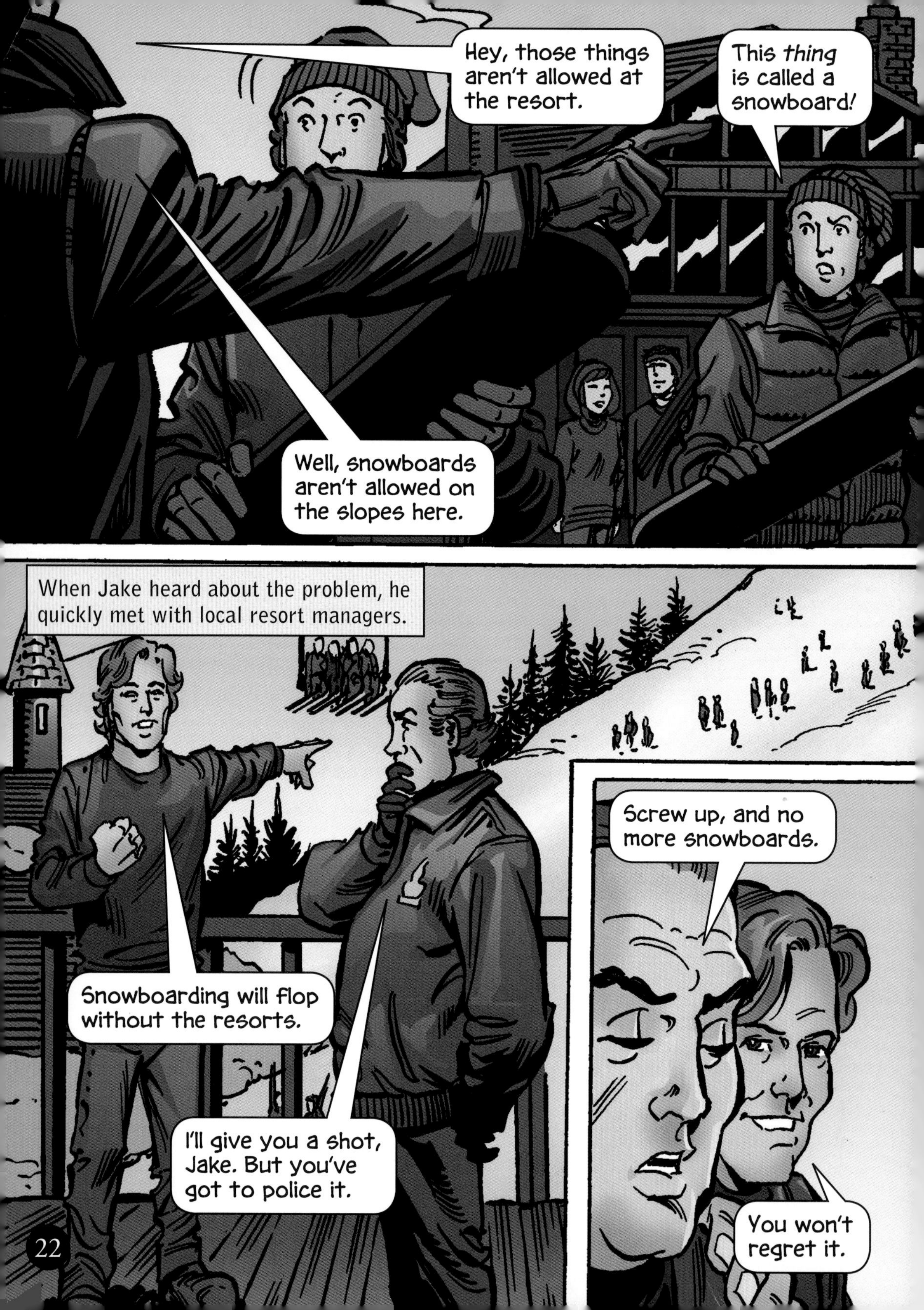
Hey, those things aren't allowed at the resort.
This *thing* is called a snowboard!
Well, snowboards aren't allowed on the slopes here.
When Jake heard about the problem, he quickly met with local resort managers.
Snowboarding will flop without the resorts.
I'll give you a shot, Jake. But you've got to police it.
Screw up, and no more snowboards.
You won't regret it.

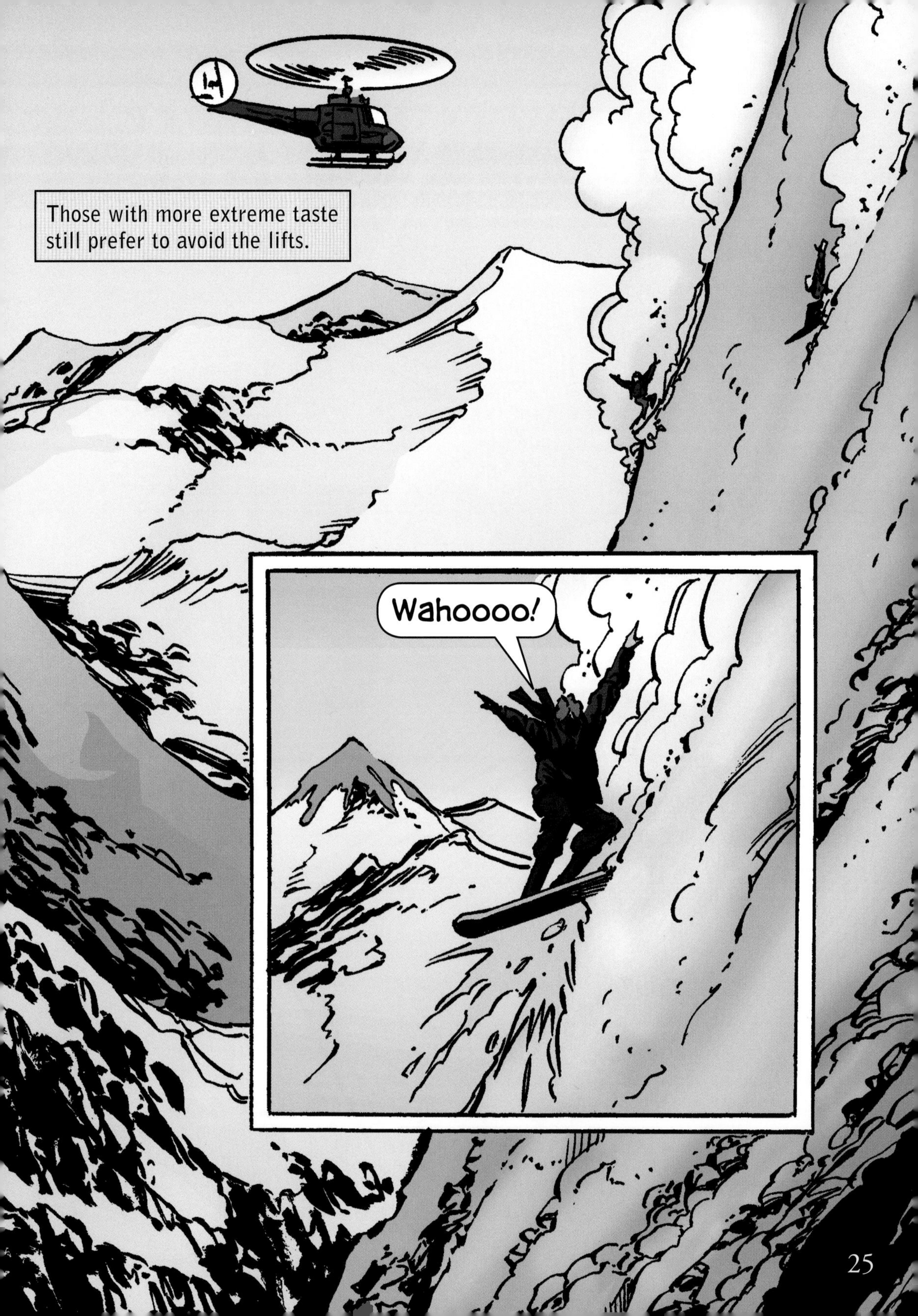
Those with more extreme taste still prefer to avoid the lifts.
Wahoooo!

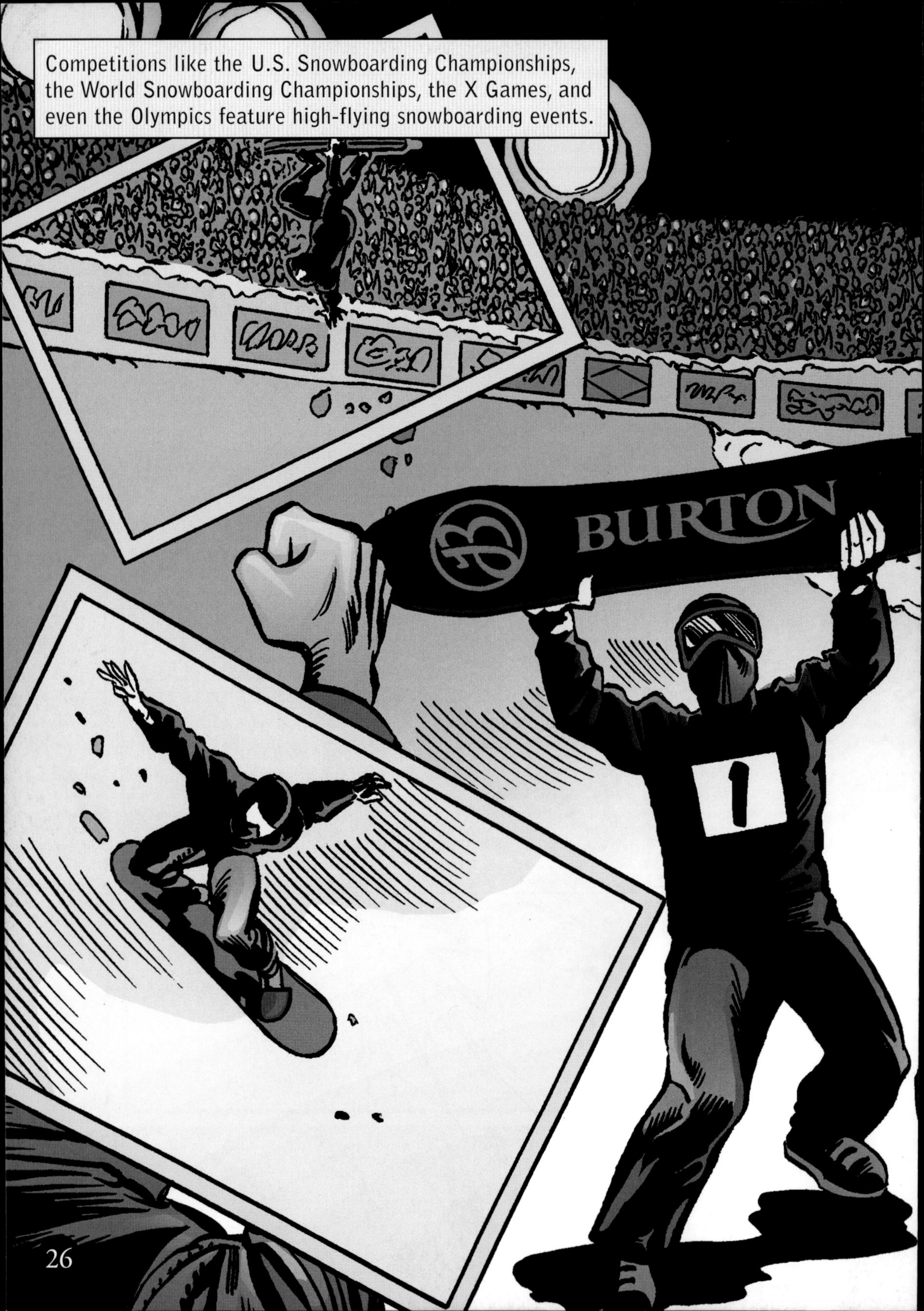
Competitions like the U.S. Snowboarding Championships, the World Snowboarding Championships, the X Games, and even the Olympics feature high-flying snowboarding events.
BURTON
1

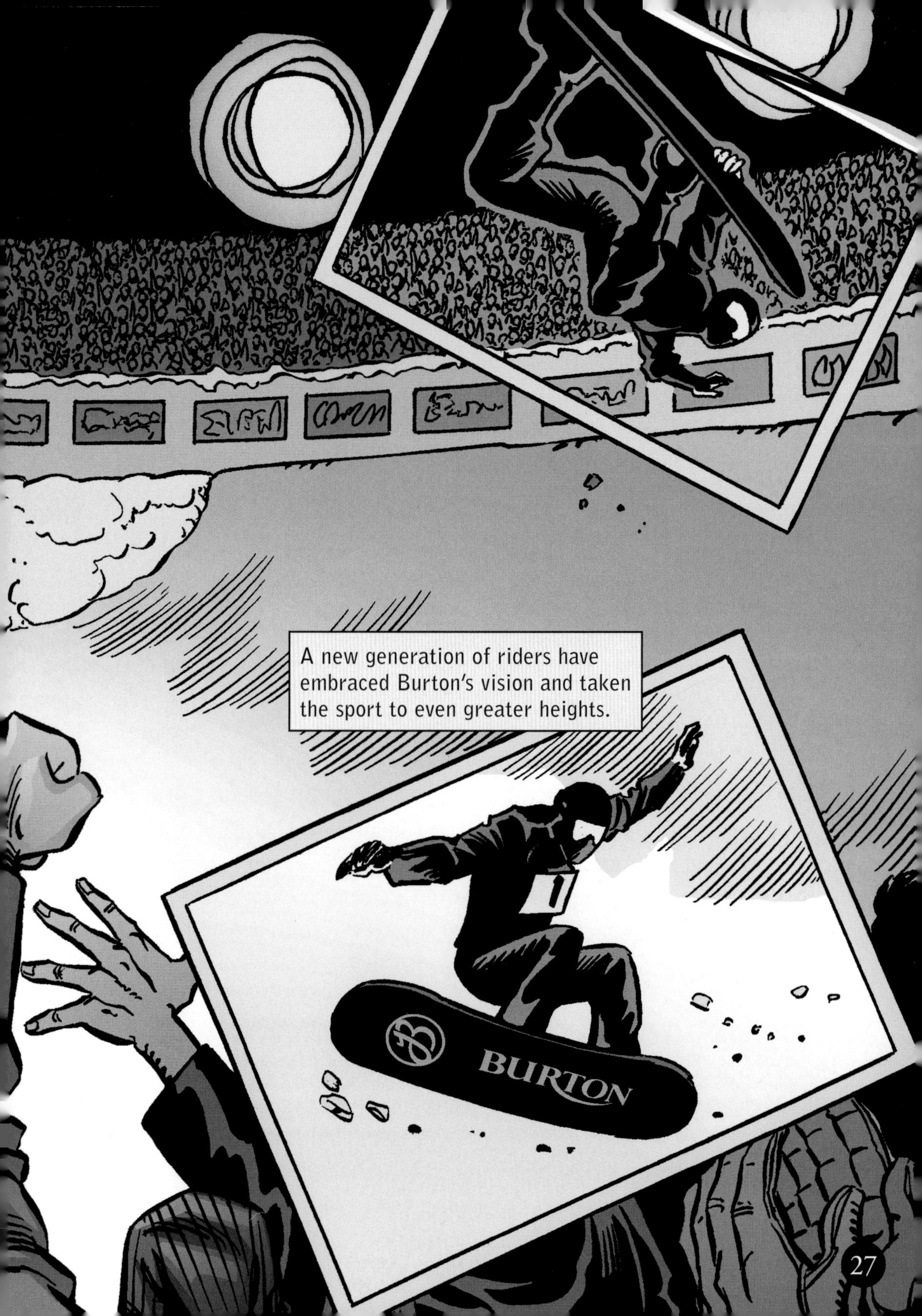
A new generation of riders have embraced Burton's vision and taken the sport to even greater heights.
BURTON

MORE ABOUT BURTON AND SNOWBOARDS

* Jake Burton Carpenter was born in New York City, New York, on April 29, 1954. He spent most of his early years living in Cedarhurst, New York.

* Jake doesn't claim to have invented the first snowboard. In fact, no one knows who did. Some believe people have been riding homemade boards since the 1920s. Others argue that a man named Vern Wicklund made the first known board. A recently discovered film shows Wicklund riding down a Chicago hill in 1939.

* Most people agree that Sherman Poppen invented the first successful snowboard, called the Snurfer. On Christmas Day 1965, Poppen bound two skis together in his Muskegon, Michigan, garage. He invented the toy for his daughter but soon started selling them across the country. Eventually, Poppen sold nearly a million Snurfers.

* Other snowboard pioneers include Dimitrije Milovich, Chris Sanders, Chuck Barfoot, and Tim Sims. Many of their developments made the snowboard an even better product. Milovich was the first to experiment with metal edges. He went on to create Winterstick Snowboard company. In 1985, Sims introduced the first freestyle board, which had a rounded tail.

28

- In 1985, only 7 percent of all ski resorts allowed snowboards. But as more riders passed up backcountry powder for the ski hill snow, Jake made changes to his board. In 1980, he introduced the Performer Elite. This board was made from a special material and had metal edges to handle icy conditions.

- Today, almost 8 million Americans of all ages enjoy the sport of snowboarding. Nearly every resort in the United States now welcomes these riders.

- Snowboarding became an official Olympic sport at the 1998 Winter Games in Nagano, Japan. Only four years later, snowboarding was one of the most popular Olympic events. During the 2002 Olympics in Salt Lake City, Utah, thousands of fans cheered the U.S. team to a medal sweep in the halfpipe.

- At the 2006 Winter Olympics, Burton Snowboards sponsored five of eight American riders, including gold medalists Shaun White and Hannah Teter.

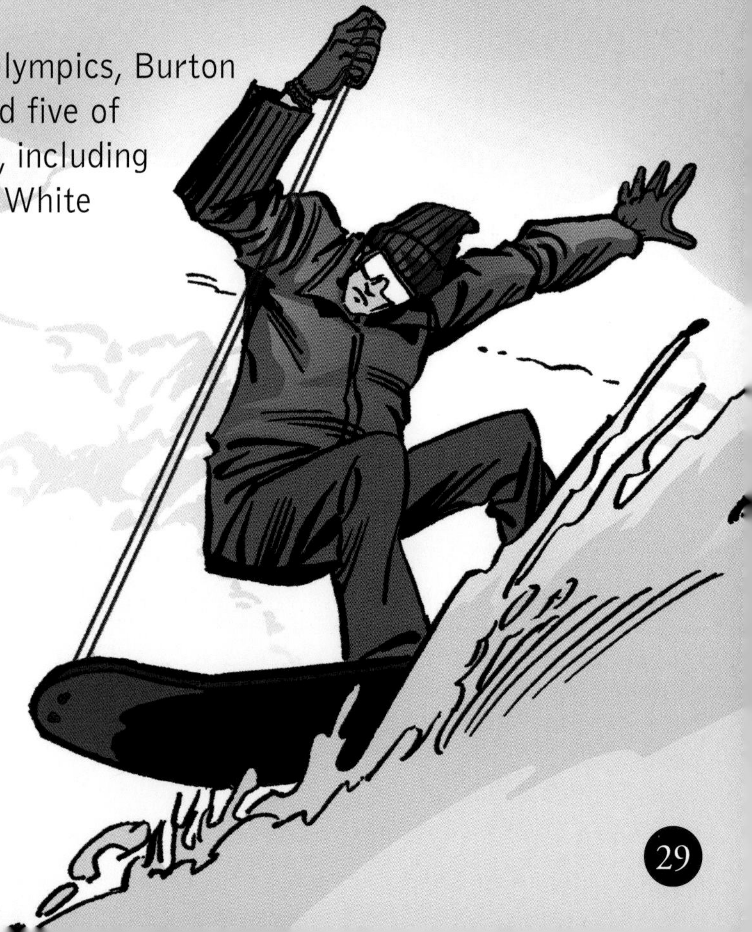

GLOSSARY

binding (BINE-ding)—a fastening for holding the boot firmly on the snowboard

customized (KUHSS-tuh-mized)—changed to suit the needs of an individual

economics (ek-uh-NOM-iks)—the study of the way money, goods, and services are made and used in society

fiberglass (FYE-bur-glass)—a strong material made from thin threads of glass

prototype (PROH-tuh-tipe)—the first version of an invention that tests an idea to see if it will work

INTERNET SITES

FactHound offers a safe, fun way to find Internet sites related to this book. All of the sites on FactHound have been researched by our staff.

Here's how:
1. Visit *www.facthound.com*
2. Choose your grade level.
3. Type in this book ID **0736864814** for age-appropriate sites. You may also browse subjects by clicking on letters, or by clicking on pictures and words.
4. Click on the **Fetch It** button.

FactHound will fetch the best sites for you!

READ MORE

Brown, Gillian C. P. *Snowboarding*. X-treme Outdoors. New York: Children's Press, 2003.

Firestone, Mary. *Extreme Halfpipe Snowboarding Moves.* Behind the Moves. Mankato, Minn.: Capstone Press, 2004.

Gifford, Clive. *Snowboarding*. Adrenalin! North Mankato, Minn.: Chrysalis Education, 2006.

Woods, Bob. *Snowboarding.* Kids' Guides. Chanhassen, Minn.: Child's World, 2005.

BIBLIOGRAPHY

Brisick, Jamie. *Have Board, Will Travel: The Definitive History of Surf, Skate, and Snow.* New York: HarperEntertainment, 2004.

Burton Snowboards Online. http://www.burton.com

Howe, Susanna. *Sick: A Cultural History of Snowboarding.* New York: St. Martin's Griffin, 1998.

Reed, Rob. *The Way of the Snowboarder.* New York: H.N. Abrams, 2005.

INDEX